ADHD
After

Workbook for Women

Strategies for Reclaiming Focus, Boosting Self-Esteem, and Building Stronger Relationships

Ava Counsel's

"For someone like me, who's very scattered, ADHD is like, 'This is my normal.' It's taken time to figure out how to manage it, but it's part of who I am." — Zooey Deschanel

Copyright   **2024 Ava Counsel's**

This book is a work of non-fiction and is based on the research and experiences of the author. Some individuals' names and personal details have been changed to protect their privacy.

Acknowledgement

I am profoundly thankful to **_Dr. Vivian Conwell_** for his invaluable guidance.

I sincerely appreciate **_Dr. Angela Daniels_** for her constant encouragement.

I want to recognize the significant contributions of **Frank** and **Michael.**

Lastly, I extend my deepest thanks to **_Parker (My husband)_** for his steadfast love and support.

About the Author

Ava Parker is a certified professional counselor with extensive experience aiding various client demographics. Over the course of twenty-five years, her focus has been on supporting women and adults in managing anxiety and enhancing self-esteem.

Her journey began with establishing a private counseling practice in the early 2000s, which later evolved into a group practice in 2005. Ava is dedicated to employing a collaborative, holistic, and compassionate methodology in her therapeutic work. Additionally, she holds certification as a Clini-Coach®, guiding women in cultivating confidence and self-love to fortify their personal connections.

Other Books by this same author includes:

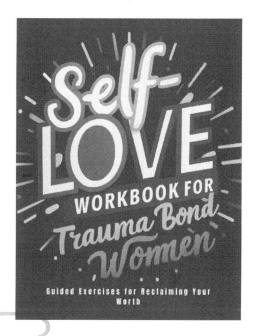

V

Table
Of Contents

How To Use This Workbook

Begin with Self-Reflection: Set aside quiet time to reflect on your own attachment experiences. This will allow you to engage more deeply with the material.

Read Each Chapter Thoughtfully: Go through each chapter at your own pace, taking time to fully grasp the concepts and how they relate to your life.

Complete the Exercises: After reading, participate in the exercises. These are designed to help you explore your thoughts, emotions, and behaviors connected to avoidant attachment.

Journal Your Reflections: Use the provided space to write down your thoughts, insights, and any patterns you observe while completing the exercises.

Practice Regularly: Consistency is essential. Set aside time each week to work on the exercises, even if it's just for a few minutes each day.

Reflect and Revisit: Occasionally review your notes and completed exercises. Reflect on your progress and how your understanding of avoidant attachment has developed.

Apply Your Insights: Start incorporating the insights and strategies you've learned into your daily life. Pay attention to how your relationships and interactions shift as you grow.

Return as Needed: This workbook is a resource for continuous growth. Revisit sections whenever your understanding expands or when new challenges come up.

"Sometimes people with ADHD see things others don't. They can bring a different perspective, and that's a strength." — Ty Pennington

Introduction

Imagine feeling as though your creative spark is fading despite your undeniable talent. For Nina, a 44-year-old graphic designer from Seattle, this was her daily reality.

Although she had always been celebrated for her innovative designs, she struggled with productivity, missed deadlines, and a growing sense of dissatisfaction. Her professional life, once a source of pride, had become a relentless source of stress.

Nina's challenges began in childhood but went unnoticed and undiagnosed for decades. As a girl, she was often described as disorganized, forgetful, and easily distracted—traits that were brushed off as quirks or a lack of discipline.

Teachers and family members would remark on her difficulties with completing tasks and staying focused, but the idea that these issues might be indicative of a deeper problem was never considered.

Her struggles continued into adulthood, manifesting as difficulty meeting deadlines, chronic procrastination, and a persistent feeling of being overwhelmed.

Despite her best efforts, she found it hard to maintain organization and balance in her professional and personal life. She often questioned why she couldn't keep up, feeling that her challenges were a personal failing rather than symptoms of a condition.

It wasn't until her early 40s, after a series of failed attempts to address her mounting issues on her own, that Nina sought a formal diagnosis.

The ADHD diagnosis was both a relief and a revelation. It explained the lifelong patterns of disorganization and distractibility she had experienced but also highlighted the difficulties of navigating a diagnosis later in life.

Many women, like Nina, are often diagnosed with ADHD much later than men, partly due to the different ways symptoms can present in women and the tendency for their symptoms to be masked or misattributed to other causes.

As her therapist, I helped Nina confront and manage these challenges with targeted strategies. We worked on implementing time management techniques, organizational tools, and mindfulness practices tailored to her specific needs.

Despite the progress, Nina continued to grapple with the demands of her job and daily life, as ADHD had long shaped her professional and personal experiences.

Amidst these struggles, Nina rediscovered an old passion—illustrating children's books. This project had been a dream of hers since childhood, a dream she had set aside as her symptoms grew more pronounced.

6

Reconnecting with this passion provided her with a renewed sense of purpose and a creative outlet that helped mitigate some of the frustrations of her everyday life.

Nina's project of illustrating a children's book focused on ADHD awareness became a pivotal moment. It allowed her to channel her creative energy into something meaningful while applying the coping strategies we developed.

The book's success, marked by a successful crowdfunding campaign and a publishing contract, was a significant personal and professional achievement.

The book's launch event in Seattle was a celebration of Nina's accomplishments and served as a platform for discussing ADHD and self-acceptance. The event, which included a workshop on ADHD awareness, showcased her journey and the impact of her renewed focus.

Nina's recognition from a local mental health organization further highlighted her resilience and the positive influence she had made in her community.

In the pages of this workbook, you will find a comprehensive guide designed to support women navigating ADHD later in life.

This book offers practical strategies for reclaiming focus, boosting self-esteem, and enhancing relationships. Through personal stories, evidence-based techniques, and actionable exercises, you will explore ways to harness your strengths, manage your symptoms, and build a fulfilling life.

As you work through these pages, my hope is that you will find guidance, inspiration, and the tools needed to transform your challenges into opportunities for growth and success.

Here's a simple Yes/No questionnaire designed to help you assess whether they might have ADHD.

Please note, this questionnaire is not a diagnostic tool but can serve as a starting point for discussion with a healthcare professional.

Do you often find it difficult to stay focused on tasks, even those you find interesting?
- *Yes*
- *No*

Do you frequently make careless mistakes in work or other activities due to a lack of attention to detail?
- *Yes*
- *No*

Do you often feel restless or find it hard to stay seated in situations where it's expected?
- *Yes*
- *No*

Do you frequently interrupt others or have difficulty waiting for your turn in conversations or activities?
- *Yes*
- *No*

Do you often misplace items necessary for tasks or activities, such as keys, documents, or your phone?
- *Yes*
- *No*

Do you find it challenging to follow through with tasks or commitments, even if you initially intend to complete them?
- *Yes*
- *No*

Do you often feel overwhelmed by everyday tasks and responsibilities, leading to procrastination?
- *Yes*
- *No*

Do you have trouble organizing tasks and activities, often resulting in missed deadlines or disarray?

- *Yes*
- *No*

Do you find it difficult to stay on topic during conversations or meetings, frequently drifting off or losing focus?

- *Yes*
- *No*

Do you often feel mentally exhausted by the end of the day due to the effort it takes to stay focused or organized?

- *Yes*
- *No*

Have you experienced similar symptoms since childhood, though they may have been overlooked or misunderstood?

- *Yes*
- *No*

Chapter 1

UNDERSTANDING ADHD IN WOMEN OVER 40

It took me 45 years to get diagnosed with ADHD. That's 45 years of feeling like a failure in life, even when I was achieving things by societal standards." - Grace

This powerful quote reflects the experience of many women who only find out they have ADHD later in life. They might have spent years, or even decades, feeling inadequate and like they weren't reaching their full potential, despite having success in some areas.

They often feel trapped in a cycle of fluctuating emotions and productivity.

Why does this happen? Why do so many women only realize the cause of their lifelong difficulties in their 40s or later? The answer lies in the complex and often misunderstood nature of ADHD, particularly in how it manifests in women.

Traditionally, ADHD was thought to mainly affect young boys who were hyperactive and impulsive.

This limited view led to many girls and women being misdiagnosed or overlooked, as their symptoms often differed and were dismissed as something else.

While some women with ADHD do display the classic symptoms of hyperactivity and impulsiveness, many others show a more internalized form of the disorder.

This includes inattentiveness, disorganization, forgetfulness, and emotional regulation issues. These traits are often mistaken for personality flaws or a lack of effort.

As a result, many women with ADHD grow up feeling they're simply "lazy," "scatterbrained," or "not trying hard enough." They might develop complex coping strategies to hide their struggles, sometimes at great personal expense.

They may become perfectionists, people-pleasers, or workaholics, only to experience burnout. Relationships can be challenging due to issues with communication, emotional control, and consistency.

For some women, the impact of ADHD becomes more intense as they reach their 40s and beyond.

Hormonal changes, career shifts, and parenting responsibilities can worsen existing symptoms and make it harder to keep up the appearance of normalcy. Old coping methods might no longer be effective, leading to increased stress, anxiety, and even depression.

As awareness and research on ADHD in women grow, more women are now receiving accurate diagnoses and finding the support and treatment they need.

They are discovering that their difficulties are not personal failures but a neurobiological difference that can be managed with the right strategies and tools.

EVOLUTION OF ADHD

For many women, discovering they have ADHD isn't a sudden realization at age 40. Rather, it's a lifelong journey that may have been misunderstood, overlooked, or even dismissed for many years.

The signs of ADHD were likely present in childhood, but they often differed from the typical image of a hyperactive boy. For girls, ADHD often shows up in subtler ways, making it easier to miss or misinterpret.

As children, girls with ADHD might appear to be daydreamers, lost in their own thoughts instead of disrupting the classroom. They might be labeled as "*chatty*" or "*spacey*" rather than "*hyperactive.*"

Their struggles with organization and time management might be seen as laziness or carelessness, rather than symptoms of a neurological difference.

Emotional intensity, often marked by anxiety or mood swings, might be written off as "*drama*" or being "*overly sensitive.*"

15

As these girls reach adolescence and young adulthood, their challenges can become more pronounced. The complexity of school and social demands requires advanced executive function skills, which they might lack.

This can lead to trouble keeping up with assignments, managing schedules, and handling social interactions. The pressure to meet societal expectations can be overwhelming for young women with ADHD, who may feel like they're always falling short.

To deal with these difficulties, many women with ADHD create elaborate **"masking"** strategies. They might overcompensate by becoming excessively organized or taking on too many responsibilities.

They might mimic social cues and behaviors, despite it being draining. They may strive for perfection, aiming to prove their worth through academic or professional achievements.

While these strategies can offer short-term relief, they can also be exhausting and unsustainable. Over time, they may lead to burnout, anxiety, depression, and a drop in self-esteem.

The constant effort to hide or suppress ADHD symptoms can leave women feeling like they're living a double life, unable to be their true selves.

The transition to midlife can be especially challenging for women with ADHD. Hormonal changes related to perimenopause and menopause can worsen existing symptoms or even bring on new ones.

Fluctuating estrogen levels can impact attention, focus, and emotional regulation, leading to increased distractibility, forgetfulness, and mood swings.

For women who have masked their ADHD symptoms for years, these changes can be particularly disorienting as their old coping methods may suddenly fail.

17

Additionally, midlife often introduces its own set of transitions and challenges, such as career changes, empty nests, aging parents, and health concerns.

For women with ADHD, who may already struggle with time management, organization, and decision-making, these new stresses can feel overwhelming.

It's important to recognize that not all women with ADHD will follow the same path. Some may have been diagnosed and treated early, while others might not realize their symptoms until later in life. Some may have developed effective coping strategies that continue to help them, while others might face ongoing difficulties.

Understanding the common ways ADHD manifests in girls and young women, along with the effects of masking and hormonal changes, is key to recognizing and addressing this often-misunderstood condition. By acknowledging the unique challenges faced by women with ADHD throughout their lives, we can offer better support, treatment, and resources to help them succeed.

18

EXERCISES

Create a Timeline of Your Life

Step 1: Gather Materials

- Obtain a large sheet of paper or a digital tool (like a timeline software or spreadsheet).
- Gather writing tools: pens, markers, or a keyboard for typing.

Step 2: Draw Your Timeline

- On Paper: Draw a horizontal line across the middle of the sheet. This will serve as your timeline.
- Digitally: Create a horizontal line using your chosen software. Ensure you have space to add events along the line.

Step 3: Mark Key Life Stages

- Divide the timeline into significant stages of your life (e.g., childhood, adolescence, early adulthood, and current age).
- Label each stage clearly to provide context.

Step 4: Identify and Add Key Events

- Reflect on major life events, both positive and negative. These might include:
  - Personal milestones: Birthdays, graduations, marriage, births of children, etc.
  - Challenges: Moving to a new city, job changes, health issues, etc.
  - Successes: Achievements in your career, personal accomplishments, overcoming difficulties, etc.
  - Add these events to the timeline at appropriate points.

Step 5: Note Patterns and Recurring Themes

- As you review your timeline, look for patterns or recurring themes. For example:
  - ADHD Symptoms: Note any events that may have been influenced by ADHD symptoms such as disorganization, impulsivity, or difficulties with focus.
  - Emotional Responses: Identify how you reacted to various events and if there are any patterns in how you handle challenges or successes.

20

- Mark these patterns on the timeline, perhaps with different colors or symbols.

Step 6: Reflect on ADHD Symptoms

- Review your timeline with ADHD symptoms in mind. Consider the following questions:
  - Have there been recurring challenges that align with typical ADHD symptoms (e.g., trouble meeting deadlines, forgetfulness)?
  - Are there specific life events that triggered or exacerbated these symptoms?
- Highlight these connections directly on your timeline.

Step 7: Analyze and Summarize

- Write a brief summary of your findings. Reflect on how understanding these patterns can help you manage ADHD symptoms more effectively.
- Consider how recognizing these patterns might influence your approach to your personal and professional life.

Step 8: Update as Needed

- Remember that your timeline is a living document. Update it periodically as you have new insights or experiences.

This exercise aims to provide insight into how ADHD may have impacted various aspects of your life and to help identify strategies to address these challenges moving forward.

Use the template below for this effect or use it as a guide to create yours.

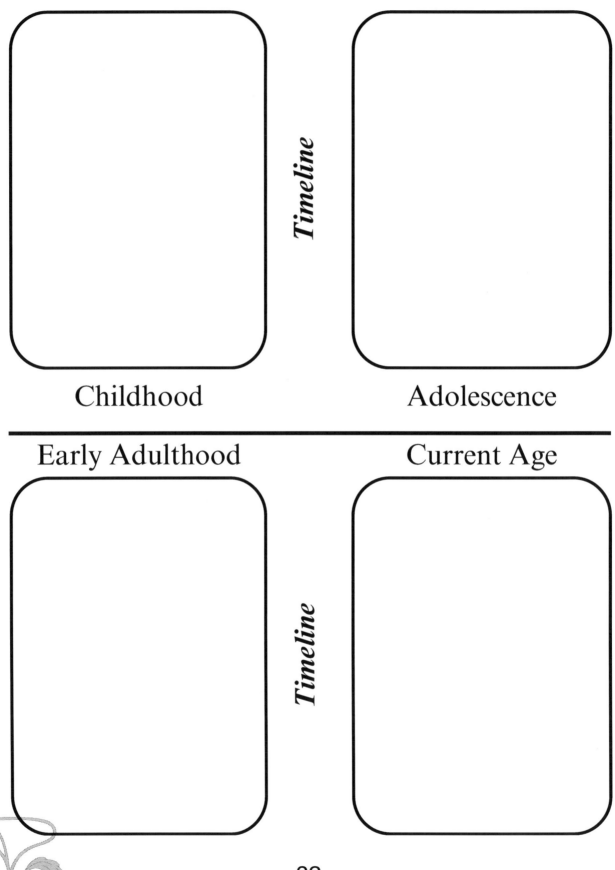

Childhood

Timeline

Adolescence

Early Adulthood

Current Age

Timeline

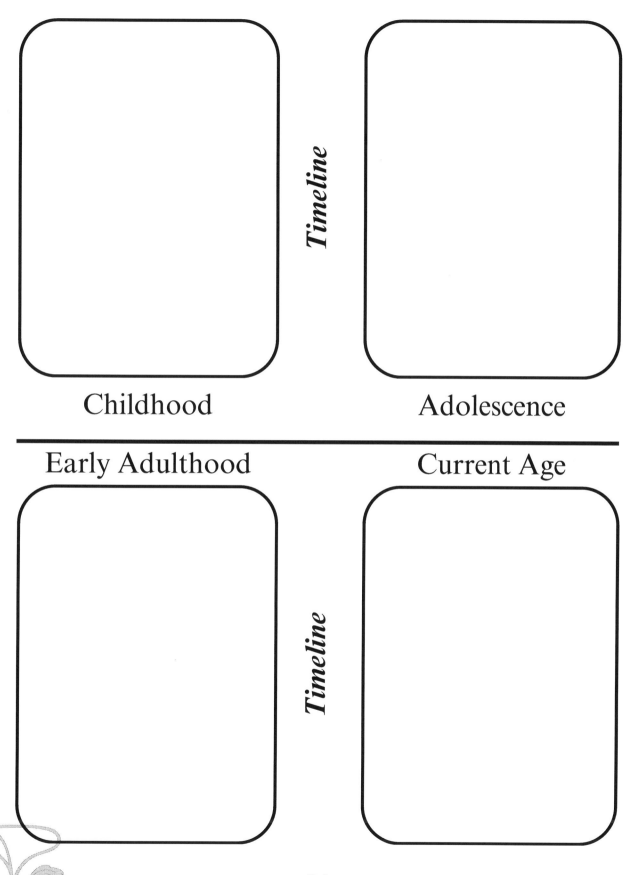

Childhood

Adolescence

Early Adulthood

Current Age

24

Timeline

Childhood

Adolescence

Early Adulthood

Current Age

Timeline

25

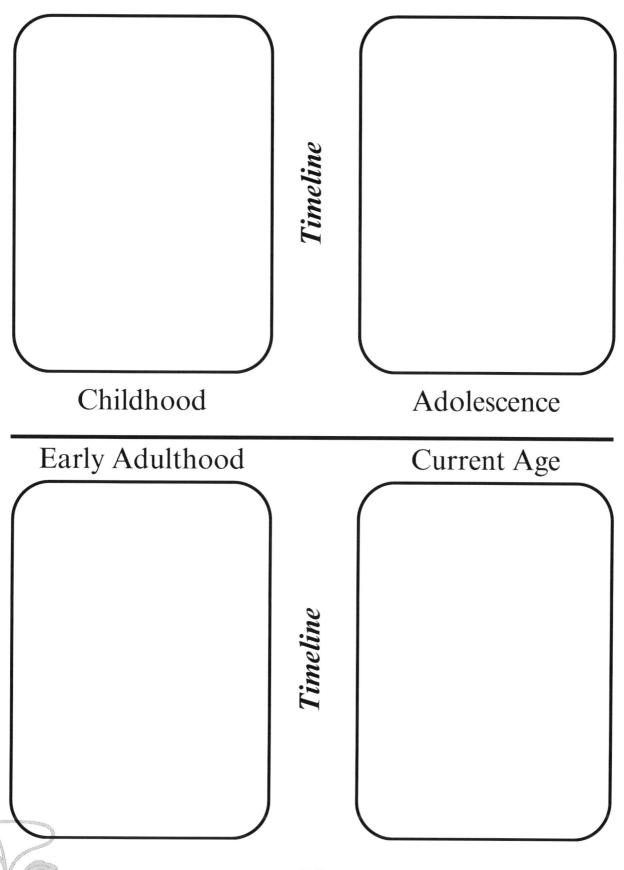

Timeline

Childhood

Adolescence

Early Adulthood

Current Age

Timeline

26

How have societal expectations or gender roles influenced my perception of myself and my struggles?

_____

_____

_____

_____

What are my biggest hopes and fears about receiving an ADHD diagnosis?

_____

_____

_____

_____

Chapter 2

REFRAMING YOUR STORY

For years, perhaps even decades, you've felt like you didn't quite fit in, struggling to navigate a world that seems to be built for minds that work differently from yours. You've been labeled as ***"too much"*** or ***"not enough,"*** with your energy dismissed as disruptive and your distractibility mistaken for a lack of focus or intelligence.

Yet now, you're on the brink of a new understanding, a fresh perspective. You're not broken or flawed—you're simply different. And that difference isn't something to hide from, but something to embrace.

ADHD isn't a disease or a disorder; it's a neurological difference—a unique way your brain processes information and interacts with the world. It's a brain wired for creativity, passion, and innovative thinking. It's a mind always searching for new experiences, connections, and meaning.

But for women, especially those over 40, this neurological difference often carries the weight of societal expectations and feelings of internalized shame.

We've been conditioned to be quiet, compliant, organized, and to follow the rules. When we fall short of these expectations, we blame ourselves, thinking we aren't trying hard enough or aren't good enough.

This self-blame can lead to years of self-doubt, anxiety, and even depression. It can show up as *perfectionism, imposter syndrome*, or a *persistent fear of failure.* It can create barriers to forming healthy relationships, building satisfying careers, or simply enjoying the present moment.

But what if we could rewrite that narrative? What if, instead of seeing ADHD as a weakness, we viewed it as a strength? What if, instead of trying to squeeze ourselves into a mold that doesn't fit, we embraced our unique wiring and designed a life that truly suits us?

This is the power of reframing. It's about shifting your mindset, questioning long-held beliefs, and creating new stories about yourself and your experiences. It's about seeing ADHD not as a setback, but as a source of creativity, passion, and resilience.

The journey starts with a simple yet profound change in perspective. It's about recognizing ADHD not as a deficit, but as a difference—a unique way of experiencing the world. It's about understanding that your brain isn't faulty, just differently wired, and this difference can be a wellspring of strength and innovation.

It's also about realizing that your challenges don't define your character or value. They're simply a byproduct of having a brain that operates outside the conventional norm. And it's about approaching those challenges with compassion and understanding, rather than judgment and shame.

SHATTERING THE MYTHS AND STIGMA

Attention-Deficit/Hyperactivity Disorder (ADHD) has long been surrounded by misconceptions and stigmatizing beliefs.

For decades, misinformation has perpetuated harmful stereotypes, causing undue hardship for those living with the condition.

Breaking these myths is not only essential for those diagnosed with ADHD but also for society at large, as it allows for a more inclusive and supportive environment.

Let's explore some of the most common myths surrounding ADHD and dismantle them one by one, replacing them with more accurate, compassionate, and evidence-based understandings.

.

Myth 1: *ADHD Isn't Real—It's Just an Excuse for Bad Behavior or Laziness*

One of the most pervasive myths is that ADHD is not a "real" condition. Some believe that individuals with ADHD are simply lazy, unmotivated, or looking for an excuse to justify disorganization or inattention. This view is not only harmful but entirely unfounded.

The Reality: ADHD is recognized as a legitimate neurodevelopmental disorder by leading medical organizations such as the American Psychiatric Association (APA) and the World Health Organization (WHO).

It is characterized by persistent patterns of inattention, hyperactivity, and impulsivity that interfere with functioning in daily life. Scientific studies show that ADHD is linked to structural and functional differences in the brain, particularly in areas related to executive function, motivation, and self-regulation.

People with ADHD often work harder than others to achieve the same outcomes because their brains process information and stimuli differently.

Myth 2: *ADHD Only Affects Children*

There is a common assumption that ADHD is a childhood disorder, one that kids simply "outgrow." While it is true that ADHD often manifests in childhood, it does not disappear with age.

The Reality: ADHD is a lifelong condition. Approximately 60% of children diagnosed with ADHD continue to experience symptoms into adulthood.

Adult ADHD can manifest differently than in childhood, with less hyperactivity and more challenges with focus, time management, and organization.

Many adults go undiagnosed because their symptoms are mistaken for stress, depression, or anxiety, particularly in women, who are often underdiagnosed due to gender biases in the understanding of ADHD.

Myth 3: *ADHD Is Overdiagnosed*

Critics often claim that ADHD is overdiagnosed, pointing to the increasing number of cases as evidence that the condition is being used as a catch-all label for any behavioral issue. Some argue that ADHD diagnosis has become trendy, leading to unnecessary treatment.

The Reality: While awareness and diagnoses have increased, this does not mean the condition is overdiagnosed. In fact, many studies suggest that ADHD is often underdiagnosed, particularly in women, minorities, and adults.

Cultural biases and lack of access to proper mental health resources mean that many people with ADHD, especially those who don't fit the "classic" hyperactive profile, may go years without a diagnosis.

Increased awareness and better diagnostic criteria have led to more accurate identification of ADHD, which was likely underrecognized in the past.

Myth 4: *Medication Is the Only Treatment for ADHD*

Many believe that the only way to manage ADHD is through medication, particularly stimulant drugs like Ritalin or Adderall. This has contributed to stigma, with some seeing medication as a crutch or even comparing it to substance abuse.

The Reality: While medication can be an effective treatment for ADHD, it is not the only option, nor is it a "magic cure."

Treatment plans for ADHD are often multifaceted and may include behavioral therapy, cognitive-behavioral interventions, coaching, mindfulness practices, and lifestyle changes such as improved sleep hygiene, regular exercise, and a structured daily routine.

Medication, when used under medical supervision, helps regulate brain chemicals involved in attention and impulse control, but many individuals benefit from combining it with other strategies that target specific challenges.

Myth 5: *People With ADHD Can't Focus on Anything*
A frequent misconception is that people with ADHD are incapable of focusing on tasks, making them unreliable or unproductive.

The Reality: People with ADHD often struggle with selective attention, meaning they may find it hard to concentrate on tasks that are monotonous or require sustained effort.

However, many individuals with ADHD experience something called "hyperfocus," where they become intensely absorbed in activities that interest them.

This can lead to prolonged periods of exceptional productivity in areas they are passionate about.

The challenge lies not in the ability to focus but in the ability to regulate and shift focus appropriately.

Myth 6: *ADHD Only Affects Boys*

Historically, ADHD has been seen as a condition that predominantly affects boys, particularly those who are hyperactive or disruptive in classroom settings. This has led to underdiagnosis and a lack of awareness about how ADHD presents in other populations, especially girls.

The Reality: ADHD affects people of all genders, but the symptoms can manifest differently.

Boys are more likely to exhibit hyperactive and impulsive behaviors, which are more noticeable in school settings, while girls often exhibit the inattentive type of ADHD, which may manifest as daydreaming, disorganization, or difficulty completing tasks.

Girls with ADHD may also develop coping strategies to mask their symptoms, such as being overly perfectionistic or people-pleasing, which can lead to a delay in diagnosis.

Myth 7: *ADHD Is a Modern Disorder Caused by Technology*

Some argue that ADHD is a byproduct of modern life, with overstimulation from technology—smartphones, social media, and video games—being blamed for the rise in attention difficulties among both children and adults.

The Reality: ADHD has been documented for over a century, long before the advent of modern technology.

While today's digital age might exacerbate attention challenges, especially in people prone to distractibility, it does not cause ADHD.

ADHD is a neurobiological disorder with a strong genetic component.

Technology can play a role in how symptoms are expressed, but it does not create the underlying brain differences associated with ADHD.

CELEBRATING YOUR UNIQUE WIRING

One of the most notable strengths of the ADHD brain is its boundless creativity. This doesn't just apply to artistic expression *(though many women with ADHD excel in creative fields)*.

It's about a mindset that is spontaneous, flexible, and unafraid to challenge the norm. Women with ADHD often see connections others might miss, generate ideas seemingly out of nowhere, and approach problems from fresh, unexpected angles.

If conventional thinking is a well-worn path, the ADHD mind is an explorer in uncharted wilderness, forging new trails and uncovering hidden treasures.

This kind of innovative, out-of-the-box thinking is invaluable in areas like entrepreneurship, marketing, design, and any profession that thrives on fresh ideas

Another superpower women with ADHD often possess is intense passion.

When something ignites their interest, they plunge in wholeheartedly, with a contagious enthusiasm.

This kind of passion can be both exhilarating and all-consuming, driving women with ADHD to achieve extraordinary things.

Passion is a powerful motivator. It's what fuels our dreams, helps us overcome obstacles, and drives us to make an impact on the world. Don't underestimate your passions—they are the very fuel that can propel you toward a life full of purpose and fulfillment.

Have you ever had a gut feeling that turned out to be completely right? That's intuition, another strength that women with ADHD frequently tap into.

While others may rely on careful analysis and logic, your instincts often give you quick, accurate reads on situations and people.

This can be a powerful asset in fields like leadership, counseling, and even investing, where making swift, intuitive decisions can have huge payoffs.

40

Intuition isn't about magic—it's about drawing on a deep well of subconscious knowledge and experience. Trust your gut, listen to your inner voice, and don't hesitate to act on what your instincts are telling you.

EXERCISES

Make a list of your strengths, talents, and unique qualities. Consider how these might be connected to your ADHD brain wiring.

Set a Calm and Focused Environment:
- Find a quiet place where you won't be interrupted.
- Keep a notebook or journal and a pen handy, or use your device if you prefer typing.

Start with a Positive Mindset:
- Take a few deep breaths and remind yourself that ADHD brings unique strengths along with its challenges.
- Focus on self-acceptance and curiosity, instead of judgment, as you explore this exercise.

List Your Strengths:
- Think about areas in your life where you excel or receive compliments from others.

- Examples of strengths might include creativity, problem-solving skills, high energy, or resilience.
- Write down at least 3 to 5 strengths. If you're having trouble, ask a close friend or family member for their input.

Identify Your Talents:

- Consider hobbies, skills, or activities that come naturally to you.
- Talents might be artistic abilities, quick thinking, or the ability to connect deeply with others.
- List at least 2 to 3 talents, acknowledging that these could be areas where your ADHD allows you to think or act differently.

Reflect on Your Unique Qualities:

- Think about qualities that make you stand out, whether in social settings, work, or creative endeavors.
- These might include a strong sense of intuition, a spontaneous sense of humor, or being adventurous.
- Jot down 2 to 3 qualities that you feel proud of, even if they seem unconventional.

43

Connect to Your ADHD Brain Wiring:

- Now, reflect on how your ADHD may contribute to these strengths, talents, and qualities. For example:
  - High energy might be linked to hyperactivity.
  - Creativity may be fueled by the ability to think outside the box.
  - Multitasking could stem from the brain's tendency to switch focus rapidly.
- Write a brief explanation of how each of your strengths, talents, or qualities may be influenced by your ADHD.

Celebrate Your Neurodiversity:

- Review your list and embrace how your ADHD shapes these positive aspects of who you are.
- End the exercise by acknowledging that your brain wiring is a source of strength and that reframing your ADHD can help you harness these qualities.

What are some of the positive aspects of my ADHD that I can embrace and celebrate?

_____

_____

_____

_____

How can I challenge negative stereotypes and biases about ADHD in myself and others?

_____

_____

_____

_____

Chapter 3
MASTERING FOCUS AND ATTENTION

Like teabags steeped in the hot water of life's challenges, women with ADHD often discover their remarkable strength and resilience through the hurdles they face. And perhaps one of the most persistent hurdles is the constant battle for focus and attention.

As a woman over 40, you've likely experienced the overwhelming sensation of being lost in a sea of thoughts—struggling to stay on task or bombarded by the endless stream of information swirling in your mind. You're not alone.

Millions of women experience the same frustrations, feeling as if they're being pulled in a thousand different directions at once. It's like trying to read a book while a marching band parades through your living room—your attention is constantly hijacked by the next shiny object, intriguing idea, or urgent task.

But here's the good news: there's hope. Despite the challenges, you can learn to harness your attention, tame your distracted mind, and reclaim your focus. It won't be easy, and it won't happen overnight, but it's absolutely possible.

The key lies in understanding how your brain works, developing strategies that play to your strengths, and embracing your unique way of processing information.

For women with ADHD, focus isn't just about willpower or discipline. It's about understanding the neurological differences that make attention and concentration more difficult.

Your brain is wired for novelty, constantly seeking stimulation, and making connections between seemingly unrelated ideas. This can be an amazing strength, fueling creativity, passion, and a love of learning. But it can also make it difficult to focus on one task or follow a linear train of thought.

Think of your brain like a high-powered engine with a faulty brake system. It's fast, agile, and capable of incredible things, but it struggles to slow down or stop when needed.

The good news is, you can learn to install new brakes. By developing strategies to regulate your attention and direct your energy where it's most needed, you can find focus and productivity without losing your natural edge.

Importantly, this isn't about suppressing your tendencies or trying to conform to a **"neurotypical"** way of focusing. It's about working with your brain, not against it. It's about embracing your cognitive style and using tools that help channel your energy in ways that are productive, creative, and satisfying.

One of the key things to understand about ADHD is that it affects much more than just your ability to focus. It impacts emotional regulation, working memory, impulse control, and your overall sense of well-being.

That's why a holistic approach to managing ADHD is essential. It's not enough to simply try harder to focus—you need to address the factors that contribute to distractibility, such as stress, anxiety, sleep deprivation, and environmental triggers.

When you take a step back and view ADHD through this broader lens, you begin to see how much potential you have.

The goal isn't to stifle the way you think; it's to craft a life that allows your mind to thrive, balancing the challenges with the strengths.

By working with your brain's natural wiring, you can reclaim your attention, embrace your creativity, and build a life filled with purpose and passion.

UNDERSTANDING THE ADHD BRAIN

The human brain is a marvel of complexity, a vast network of billions of neurons working together in synchronized harmony to shape thoughts, emotions, and actions.

Yet for women with ADHD, this delicate harmony can sometimes feel more like a chaotic mix of competing sounds. The ability to focus—a cornerstone for managing daily life—often proves elusive and frustrating.

To grasp this struggle, it helps to look beneath the surface and explore the neurological roots of attention and focus. Women with ADHD may experience differences in how their brain's attention networks function compared to those without the condition.

Research points to altered activity and structural differences in key areas, especially the *prefrontal cortex*, often considered the brain's *"command center."*

This region is critical for *executive functions* like planning, organization, decision-making, and impulse control.

A major player in this story is *dopamine*, a neurotransmitter essential for regulating attention, motivation, and reward-seeking behavior. Studies suggest that individuals with ADHD may have lower levels of dopamine in certain brain regions, which contributes to challenges with focus, sustained attention, and motivation.

A deficiency in *dopamine* makes it harder to prioritize tasks, tune out distractions, and stay engaged in activities that don't provide immediate gratification. This often explains why mundane or repetitive tasks —things that aren't instantly rewarding—feel especially draining.

A central concept in understanding these challenges is *executive function*. Think of *executive functions* as the brain's air traffic control system, directing and coordinating mental processes.

51

Tasks that require sustained attention, like reading a long article or following detailed instructions, can seem overwhelming. *Impulsivity* can prompt quick decisions or actions without fully considering the consequences.

And *working memory*—the brain's ability to hold and manipulate information—may be compromised, making it harder to remember details, follow conversations, or complete multi-step tasks.

In contrast to the common struggles with focus, many women with ADHD also experience hyperfocus—a state of intense, prolonged concentration on a particular activity.

This *hyperfocus* can be both a gift and a curse. On the positive side, when it's channeled into something of interest or passion, it can lead to extraordinary productivity and creativity. However, it can also be hard to break, leading to a tunnel vision that causes other important tasks to fall by the wayside, social interactions to be missed, or transitions between activities to become challenging.

Understanding the neurological foundations of attention and focus in ADHD isn't about labeling or pathologizing women; it's about offering a deeper insight into how their brains work.

With this knowledge, women can better appreciate the unique strengths and challenges that come with ADHD.

By recognizing how their brains are wired, they can develop strategies to embrace their strengths, manage their challenges, and lead lives that align with their natural inclinations.

STRATEGIES FOR IMPROVING CONCENTRATION AND SUSTAINED ATTENTION

For many women with ADHD, staying focused and maintaining attention can feel like a constant uphill climb. However, there are proven strategies that can help you harness your attention, direct your energy, and move toward your goals. Here's a guide to some of the most effective techniques that have been shown to work:

Mindfulness Exercises:
In the storm of daily life, the mind often defaults to autopilot, flitting from one thought to the next. *Mindfulness* is the practice of anchoring yourself in the present moment, observing your thoughts and emotions without judgment.

By cultivating mindfulness, you build a mental foundation that helps keep you focused, even when distractions pull at your attention.

Start with a simple practice like *mindful breathing*. Close your eyes, take deep breaths, and focus on the sensation of your breath entering and leaving your body. When your mind inevitably wanders (and it will), gently guide it back to your breath. This repeated redirection strengthens your ability to focus.

You can also explore *guided meditations* tailored to improving focus and attention. Many apps and online platforms offer meditation programs specifically designed to help with ADHD.

Time Management Tools:

Feeling like time is always slipping away? *Time management* is crucial, especially for women with ADHD.

One popular approach is the *Pomodoro Technique*, where you break work into 25-minute intervals of focused effort, followed by a 5-minute break. This method helps manage mental fatigue, increases productivity, and prevents burnout.

Other helpful tools include time-tracking apps, calendars, and task lists. Try different systems to see what fits best for you.

The goal isn't to become overly rigid, but rather to create a structure that complements your natural energy rhythms and enhances your ability to stay on task.

Environmental Modifications:
Your environment can have a profound effect on your ability to focus. *Clutter*, excessive noise, or uncomfortable surroundings can distract your mind and drain your mental energy.

Start by simplifying your workspace—remove anything that doesn't contribute to the task at hand. Consider investing in *noise-canceling headphones* or a white noise machine if background noise is a problem.

Ensure your workspace is well-lit and ergonomically comfortable.

Small changes can make a huge difference. For example, try positioning your desk away from windows or areas with frequent foot traffic. Experiment with natural light, as it may help boost your concentration.

Medication and Therapy:

For some women, medication can be a pivotal part of managing ADHD symptoms, especially when it comes to attention. *Stimulant medications*, such as those that increase dopamine levels, can enhance focus, reduce impulsivity, and improve executive function. However, medication isn't a one-size-fits-all solution. It's important to work closely with a healthcare provider to find the right treatment plan for you.

In addition to medication, *therapy*—especially *Cognitive Behavioral Therapy (CBT)*—can be incredibly effective. CBT helps you identify and change unhelpful thought patterns and behaviors that may be contributing to your focus issues. It can also teach you strategies to manage stress, prioritize tasks, and navigate everyday challenges.

57

Identifying and Eliminating Distractions:

Distractions are everywhere—from the constant ping of notifications to the temptation of social media.

For women with ADHD, even small distractions can be incredibly disruptive, pulling focus away from important tasks.

Begin by identifying your most common distractions. Is it your phone? Email? Social media? Once you're aware of these triggers, you can take steps to minimize their impact.

For example, try turning off notifications during work hours, placing your phone in another room, or using website blockers that limit access to distracting sites.

Creating a ***dedicated workspace*** that's free from distractions can also be helpful, as can setting specific times to check emails or engage in social media.

Setting Realistic Goals

When attention is hard to maintain, it's easy to feel overwhelmed by the sheer volume of tasks and to set unrealistic goals. Instead of aiming for perfection, ***break tasks into smaller, manageable steps.*** Celebrate your small wins along the way, and don't be afraid to adjust your goals if needed.

Remember, ***progress*** is what matters most, not perfection. Be compassionate with yourself, and don't let setbacks discourage you. With persistence, patience, and the right strategies, you can regain control over your focus and make meaningful progress toward your goals.

By embracing these strategies, you can navigate the challenges of ADHD and find ways to thrive, reclaiming your ability to focus, manage distractions, and live a fulfilling life on your terms.

EXERCISES

Step 1: Choose a Focus Technique to Experiment With

Decide on a focus method to try first. Here are three examples to consider:

- **Pomodoro Method:** Work for 25 minutes, followed by a 5-minute break. After four cycles, take a longer break (15–30 minutes).

- **Mindfulness Exercises:** Before starting a task, take 2-3 minutes to close your eyes, focus on your breath, and clear your mind. When you notice distractions while working, return your attention to the task by taking a mindful breath.

- **Timeboxing:** Set specific time blocks for each task (e.g., 1 hour to write, 30 minutes for emails). Stick to the schedule and move on to the next task when the time is up.

Step 2: Implement the Technique

Use the chosen method during a work session:

- For the Pomodoro Method, set a timer for 25 minutes, then take a 5-minute break. Repeat for 4 cycles before taking a longer break.

- For Mindfulness Exercises, start with deep breathing, and refocus your attention whenever distractions arise.

- For Timeboxing, allocate specific amounts of time for each task, and work within those limits.

Step 3: Track Your Experience

Record the following:

- How well were you able to focus?
- Did you feel more or less productive than usual?
- How often did distractions pull you away from your task?

61

Step 4: Repeat with Different Techniques

Try another focus technique for your next work session. For example:

- If you started with Pomodoro, try Timeboxing next.
- Experiment with mindfulness exercises after that.

Step 5: Evaluate the Results

After trying each method, reflect on which one worked best:

- Which technique helped you stay focused the longest?
- Which felt easiest to use?
- Did any method reduce stress or distractions more effectively?

Step 6: Adopt the Most Effective Method

Based on your experience, choose the focus method that suits you best and start incorporating it regularly into your routine. You can also adapt and combine techniques to create a system that works for you.

What are my biggest distractions and how can I minimize or eliminate them?

_____

_____

_____

_____

_____

What environmental modifications can I make to create a more focus-friendly workspace?

_____

_____

_____

_____

_____

Chapter 4

ORGANIZING YOUR LIFE AND ENVIRONMENT

A 2019 study from the *Journal of Attention Disorder*s revealed that women with ADHD experience significantly more clutter and disorganization at home compared to those without ADHD.

This isn't just a matter of personal preference or a flaw in character; it's a result of how the ADHD brain functions. The disorder affects executive functions, the mental processes responsible for tasks like planning, organizing, and prioritizing. When these functions are compromised, even basic activities like cleaning or managing a schedule can feel overwhelming.

For women over 40 with ADHD, the challenge of staying organized is often intensified by work, family, and other responsibilities.

Many of us have spent years trying to hide our struggles, constantly adjusting and compensating in ways that wear us down mentally and emotionally. By midlife, the toll of living with untreated ADHD can be substantial, leaving us feeling constantly exhausted, overwhelmed, and drained.

The first step is recognizing the unique challenges we face and learning strategies that align with how our brains work.

One common struggle for women with ADHD is feeling overwhelmed by visual clutter. Our brains are easily distracted by what's around us, making it hard to focus. A messy home or workspace can bombard us with sensory input, leading to more stress and anxiety.

Research shows that visual clutter can impair attention, working memory, and decision-making. For someone with ADHD, whose brain is already working hard to manage distractions, this can be a recipe for increased difficulty.

By understanding how ADHD impacts our ability to stay organized, we can create strategies that fit our needs. Instead of tackling a large organizing task at once, we can break it into smaller, more manageable steps.

Setting realistic goals and rewarding progress can help keep us motivated, while building routines and systems can keep us on track when distractions arise.

It's also key to remember that organization doesn't need to be flawless. Striving for perfection can backfire, making us feel even more discouraged.

Instead, focus on progress. Celebrate small achievements, learn from mistakes, and be gentle with yourself when things don't go perfectly.

DECLUTTERING YOUR MIND AND SPACE

As a woman over 40 with ADHD, your environment might often reflect the internal chaos you experience. Papers accumulate like stray thoughts, unfinished projects gather dust like abandoned plans, and constant digital pings vie for your already scattered focus.

This is no accident. A 2016 study published in the *Journal of Psychiatric Research* found a strong link between clutter and stress, particularly for those with ADHD. Essentially, physical disorder amplifies mental disarray, creating a relentless cycle of stress and frustration.

Imagine your brain as a high-performance computer. When overwhelmed by excessive visual stimuli—such as heaps of laundry, stacks of mail, and overflowing drawers—it's like running too many applications at once.

The system slows down, crashes, or struggles to focus. For women with ADHD, whose brains are already prone to distraction, clutter becomes an insurmountable challenge.

But it's not just about distraction. Clutter also stirs up a wave of negative emotions. As you look at the mess, feelings of shame, guilt, and anxiety might surface, accusing you of failure and incompetence.

These emotions drain your energy and motivation, making it harder to address the clutter, which then leads to more negative feelings—a vicious cycle that can seem never-ending.

So, what's the solution? The positive news is that decluttering your space can significantly enhance your mental clarity and emotional well-being.

It's not about achieving perfection or meeting strict standards, but about creating an environment that accommodates your ADHD brain, reduces stress, improves focus, and fosters calm.

Start with small steps. Don't attempt to clean the whole house in a single weekend. Focus on one area —such as a desk, a drawer, or a countertop—and set a timer for 15-20 minutes.

Aim to discard anything broken, unused, or unnecessary. As you clear physical clutter, you might find that your mental space starts to feel less crowded.

Develop systems that suit your needs. If you habitually leave your keys on the counter, designate a specific bowl or hook for them.

If papers pile up on your desk, consider a filing system or create a "command center" with designated trays for incoming mail, bills, and important documents. The goal is to establish routines that make maintaining order easier.

Adopt a minimalist approach. This doesn't mean living in stark surroundings with only the essentials. It means being deliberate about what you introduce into your life.

Before acquiring something new, ask yourself if it genuinely adds value or if it will simply add to the clutter. The fewer items you have, the less you'll need to manage, and the more mental space you'll have for what truly matters.

Remember, decluttering is a continuous journey, not a one-time task. As Dr. David Tolin, a psychologist who specializes in hoarding disorder, notes, ***"It's not about getting rid of everything; it's about finding a balance that works for you."***

For women with ADHD, this balance might change over time depending on personal circumstances and preferences. The key is to remain adaptable, forgiving, and open to adjusting your strategies as needed.

EXERCISES

Declutter One Area of Your Life

Objective: To experience the benefits of creating more space and order in your environment and reflect on how it impacts your well-being.

Step 1: Choose Your Area: Select an Area: Decide on one specific area of your life to declutter. It could be your desk, closet, email inbox, or any other space that feels disorganized and overwhelming.

Step 2: Set a Goal: Define the Scope: Determine what you want to achieve. For example, if you're decluttering your desk, you might aim to clear off the surface, organize papers into folders, and eliminate unnecessary items.

Step 3: Gather Supplies: Get Tools: Gather any tools you might need, such as trash bags, storage containers, or cleaning supplies.

71

Step 4: Declutter: Start Sorting: Begin by removing everything from the chosen area. For a desk, this means taking all items off the desk surface and out of drawers.

Categorize: Sort items into categories such as "Keep," "Donate," "Sell," and "Discard." For your email inbox, categorize emails into folders or labels, and decide which emails to delete or archive.

Step 5: Clean: Wipe Down: Clean the area you've just decluttered. For a desk, this involves wiping down the surface and any shelves or drawers.

Step 6: Organize: Put Items Back: Arrange the items you decided to keep in a way that maximizes space and accessibility. Use storage solutions like trays, bins, or drawer organizers if needed.

Set Up Systems: For ongoing organization, establish a system. For example, create a filing system for documents or a routine for managing emails.

Step 7: Reflect: Notice Your Feelings: Take a moment to notice how you feel about the newly organized space. Are you feeling a sense of relief, satisfaction, or calm?

Assess the Impact: Consider how this decluttering has impacted your productivity, mood, or stress levels. Reflect on any changes in how you interact with this area of your life.

Step 8: Maintain: Create a Routine: Set up a regular maintenance schedule to keep the area organized. This could be a weekly or monthly review to ensure the space remains clutter-free.

Step 9: Document Your Experience: Journal: Write down your observations and feelings about the decluttering process. This can help you track your progress and motivate you to tackle other areas in the future.

By following these steps, you'll gain practical experience in organizing and benefit from a clearer, more manageable environment.

How does physical clutter affect my mental state and ability to focus?

_____

_____

_____

_____

_____

What are my biggest challenges with organization, and what steps can I take to address them?

_____

_____

_____

_____

"I am very connected to my ADHD. I look at the positive aspects of it, like being able to multitask in ways that other people can't." — *Carrie Fisher*

Chapter 5

MANAGING MOODS AND ANXIETY

For many women, ADHD's emotional ups and downs become more intense after 40. Hormonal changes, life transitions, and years of feeling misunderstood and overwhelmed can combine to create a storm of emotional dysregulation.

Mood swings might feel sudden and severe—one moment you're full of energy and excitement, and the next, you plunge into irritation or sadness.

Anxiety may become a frequent presence, driven by worries about unmet expectations, incomplete tasks, or strained relationships.

These emotional challenges don't reflect weakness or failure; they stem from how your brain works and are a legitimate part of your experience.

Acknowledging this is the first step toward managing your emotions and reclaiming control over your well-being.

Let's explore the link between ADHD and emotional regulation. Research shows that women with ADHD are more prone to mood swings, anxiety, and depression compared to those without the condition.

This is partly due to differences in brain chemistry—specifically, neurotransmitters like dopamine and norepinephrine, which regulate both mood and attention.

But it's not just about brain chemistry. The daily difficulties of living with ADHD—staying focused, organized, and managing responsibilities—can lead to feelings of frustration, inadequacy, and overwhelm.

Struggles with time management and task completion increase stress and anxiety, while impulsivity can strain relationships and result in regretful decisions.

Additionally, women with ADHD often face unique societal pressures. Many feel the need to be the perfect spouse, mother, and professional, all while managing their ADHD symptoms.

This expectation to **_"keep it all together"_** can foster shame, guilt, and feelings of inadequacy when they inevitably fall short.

It's crucial to recognize that these emotional struggles are not your fault. You're not responsible for your brain's unique wiring or the unrealistic societal expectations you face. Understanding the causes of your emotional challenges can help you develop self-compassion and begin your healing process.

Self-awareness is a powerful tool in managing emotional dysregulation. By recognizing your emotional triggers and patterns, you can better anticipate and handle difficult situations before they get out of control.

Developing healthy coping strategies is also key. This might include regular exercise, practicing mindfulness or meditation, engaging in creative activities, or spending time outdoors. These actions can help reduce stress, boost your mood, and cultivate a sense of calm and balance.

Remember, everyone's ADHD journey is different, and what works for one person may not work for another. Don't be afraid to try various strategies until you discover what makes you feel your best.

SELF-CARE STRATEGIES FOR EMOTIONAL REGULATION

Living with ADHD as a woman over 40 can feel like riding an emotional rollercoaster. The highs often come with bursts of creativity and passion, while the lows bring overwhelm, anxiety, and sometimes even despair.

These emotional fluctuations are a hallmark of ADHD, but they don't have to run your life. With the right strategies, you can learn to regulate your emotions, build resilience, and create a more balanced, fulfilling existence.

Here are some evidence-based coping mechanisms to help manage the emotional challenges of ADHD:

Relaxation Techniques: When stress and overwhelm hit, relaxation techniques can offer quick relief. Deep breathing is one of the simplest and most effective tools. By focusing on your breath, you can calm your mind and body, slowing the racing thoughts and intense emotions.

80

Try inhaling deeply through your nose for a count of four, holding for four, and exhaling through your mouth for another four.

Progressive muscle relaxation, where you tense and then release different muscle groups, is another powerful tool. This practice helps release physical tension and brings your attention back to the present. Mindfulness exercises, such as meditation or yoga, can also be beneficial, increasing your awareness of emotions and giving you space to respond rather than react.

Journaling: Writing down your thoughts and feelings can be incredibly therapeutic. Journaling allows you to process emotions, gain clarity, and track patterns that contribute to distress.

It's a space where you can freely express frustrations, anxieties, and hopes without judgment. Over time, you might begin to notice triggers that lead to emotional dysregulation and can brainstorm ways to handle them more effectively.

Consider mood tracking in your journal as well. Jot down what triggers a particular emotion, and how you responded. This practice increases self-awareness, a critical skill for managing ADHD.

Exercise: Physical activity is a game changer when it comes to emotional regulation. Exercise releases endorphins—natural chemicals that improve your mood and alleviate stress, anxiety, and depression.

You don't need to run marathons to see the benefits; something as simple as a brisk 30-minute walk can make a significant difference. Find an activity you enjoy, whether it's dancing, yoga, swimming, or even gardening. The goal is to move your body in ways that feel good and are sustainable for you.

Seek Professional Help: While self-care strategies like journaling and exercise are valuable, they may not be enough when facing deeper emotional challenges.

If you find yourself consistently struggling, seeking professional help is crucial.

Cognitive-behavioral therapy (CBT) is particularly effective for women with ADHD, as it focuses on identifying and challenging negative thought patterns that contribute to emotional dysregulation.

Medication is another option for some women, helping to stabilize mood and reduce emotional intensity. It's important to consult with a healthcare provider to explore options tailored to your unique needs.

Self-Care and Boundaries: Taking care of your emotional well-being isn't selfish—it's necessary. Make time for activities that nurture you, like spending time outdoors, reading, listening to music, or soaking in a bath.

Prioritize relationships that uplift you and don't be afraid to set boundaries with those who drain your energy. Healthy boundaries allow you to protect your mental space and avoid emotional exhaustion.

EXERCISES

Develop a Self-Care Toolkit

Step 1: Identify Your Triggers

- Write down situations, thoughts, or people that tend to increase your stress, anxiety, or emotional overwhelm.
- Reflect on how these triggers affect you both physically and emotionally (e.g., tight muscles, racing thoughts).

Step 2: Recognize Your Current Coping Strategies

- Make a list of ways you typically deal with stress and anxiety, whether helpful or unhelpful.
- Assess if your current methods (e.g., venting to friends, avoiding tasks, overeating) are supporting or hurting your emotional well-being.

Step 3: Explore Calming Activities

- Brainstorm activities that calm you when you feel stressed or anxious. These can include:
  - Deep breathing exercises

- Meditation or mindfulness practices
- Gentle stretches or yoga
- Taking a walk in nature
- Listening to music
- Journaling your thoughts

Step 4: Add Activities that Boost Positive Emotions

- Think of activities that uplift your mood and make you feel good. These may include:
  - Creative outlets (painting, writing, playing an instrument)
  - Social activities (spending time with supportive friends or family)
  - Engaging hobbies or interests (reading, cooking, gardening)

Step 5: Create a "Quick Relief" List

- List 3-5 activities from Steps 3 and 4 that can provide quick relief when you're feeling overwhelmed. For example:
  - 5-minute breathing exercise
  - Texting a friend
  - Listening to a favorite song

85

- Ensure these activities are easy to do and require minimal setup.

Step 6: Build Your Long-Term Wellness Plan

- Choose activities that you can integrate into your daily or weekly routine to maintain emotional balance. These might include:
- Regular exercise or yoga sessions
- Keeping a gratitude journal
- Scheduling time for relaxation or hobbies

Step 7: Write It Down

- Compile all of the strategies and activities into one list or document.
- You can break the list into sections, such as "Immediate Stress Relief," "Daily Wellness Habits," and "Mood Boosters."

Step 8: Personalize Your Toolkit

- Add any additional items that are unique to you, such as favorite quotes, affirmations, or even small objects (e.g., stress ball) that help calm you.
- Consider making a physical or digital version of your toolkit that's easy to access.

Step 9: Practice and Review

- Use your self-care toolkit when stress or anxiety arises, and keep practicing these activities regularly.
- Periodically review and adjust the list as your needs evolve or you discover new self-care strategies.

This toolkit will become your go-to resource for managing moods, alleviating anxiety, and nurturing emotional well-being.

How do my ADHD symptoms affect my emotional well-being and mood regulation?

_____

_____

_____

_____

What additional self-care strategies could I incorporate into my routine to better support my emotional health?

_____

_____

_____

_____

"*Having ADHD doesn't make you less than; it makes you unique. You just need to learn how to manage it, not let it manage you.*" — *Mel Robbins*

Chapter 6

FINDING YOUR FLOW

The ability to think creatively, make unexpected connections, and approach problems from different perspectives is a gift that has driven many groundbreaking achievements.

For women over 40 with ADHD, this creative potential may have been stifled by the challenges of daily life.

Perhaps as a child, you were told to **"calm down"** or **"focus,"** leading you to believe that your unique way of thinking was flawed. But what if those very traits were actually your strengths?

The concept of **"flow,"** where you become completely immersed in an activity and time seems to disappear, is particularly relevant to women with ADHD.

While a wandering mind may seem like a disadvantage, it can become a source of inspiration and innovation when directed appropriately. Achieving flow allows you to tap into a deep sense of energy, focus, and fulfillment.

Flow isn't limited to artistic pursuits, though it may arise in writing, painting, or playing music. It can also be found in activities like gardening, cooking, or hands-on projects.

Even tasks like solving complex problems, analyzing data, or brainstorming can bring about flow when they challenge and engage your mind, letting you lose yourself in the moment.

However, women with ADHD often face difficulties in reaching this state due to distractions, impulsivity, and trouble maintaining focus. Finding flow requires experimentation, trying different strategies, and being open to new ways of thinking. A supportive environment that encourages exploration and provides structure can also help facilitate this process.

91

Take Mabel, for instance, a 45-year-old woman who was recently diagnosed with ADHD. For years, she struggled with multiple projects, never quite finishing any.

Writing was her passion, but staying focused for long periods felt impossible. After her diagnosis, she began to better understand her brain and started experimenting with strategies to manage her ADHD.

Setting small, achievable goals, breaking tasks into manageable steps, and using a timer helped her stay focused and avoid feeling overwhelmed.

Mabel also created a distraction-free workspace and scheduled regular writing sessions, which made it easier to slip into a flow state. Over time, she came to view her ADHD as a strength rather than a limitation. Her unique way of thinking and ability to make connections between unrelated ideas fueled her creativity and led to breakthroughs in her writing.

EMBRACING YOUR CREATIVE BRAIN

The ADHD brain isn't just prone to wandering—it's constantly wondering, questioning, and exploring. It thrives on making connections between seemingly unrelated ideas.

This is known as **"divergent thinking,"** a cognitive style that contrasts with the more structured, linear approach often prioritized in school or work environments.

While linear thinking aims for one right solution, divergent thinking generates multiple ideas and perspectives. This ability to think outside the box is invaluable in areas that demand originality and innovation.

Take Simone, a 45-year-old graphic designer who struggled with the routine nature of her job. After being diagnosed with ADHD, she realized her tendency to "zone out" during meetings wasn't due to

disinterest but because her brain processed information differently. She embraced this unique thinking style and incorporated spontaneity and improvisation into her work. The result? A series of award-winning designs celebrated for their creativity and emotional impact.

Simone's story is not unique. Many women with ADHD have found success in creative fields like writing, music, entrepreneurship, and the arts.

What sets them apart isn't just their ADHD but their ability to use it as a strength. They channel hyperfocus into creative energy bursts, use impulsivity to fuel innovation, and celebrate their distinct perspectives.

Of course, ADHD's link to creativity comes with challenges.

Traits that encourage creativity can also lead to struggles with organization, follow-through, and self-regulation.

For many women, the creative process feels like a rollercoaster—marked by exhilarating highs and frustrating lows. However, with the right tools and strategies, these challenges can be managed, allowing creativity to flourish.

Equally important is creating an environment that supports creativity. This might mean setting aside dedicated time for creative activities, minimizing distractions, and surrounding yourself with inspiration. It could also mean embracing a flexible schedule or exploring careers that allow you to express creativity authentically.

The creative journey for women with ADHD is rarely smooth, but it's filled with possibility.

By embracing their neurodiversity, recognizing their strengths, and managing their challenges, these women can access a deep well of creativity that enhances both their own lives and the world around them.

Curiosity is a powerful way to unlock creative potential. Ask questions, explore new ideas, and challenge conventional thinking.

Don't be afraid to experiment, take risks, and embrace the unexpected. The ADHD brain is naturally drawn to exploration, so follow your curiosity wherever it leads.

Lastly, it's important to embrace imperfection. Many women with ADHD struggle with perfectionism and feel overwhelmed by the pressure to meet impossible standards.

However, creativity thrives in environments where mistakes are welcomed as part of the learning process. Accept the unpredictable, messy nature of creativity and allow yourself to make mistakes. Remember, many groundbreaking ideas have emerged from accidents and unexpected outcomes.

EXERCISES

Step 1: Create a Quiet, Focused Environment

Find a comfortable space where you can focus without distractions. You want to be in a mindset that encourages creativity and self-reflection

Step 2: Brainstorm Activities That Spark Interest

On a blank piece of paper or in a journal, start brainstorming a list of activities, hobbies, or interests that make you curious, excited, or energized. Think about:

- Activities you've enjoyed in the past but might have stopped doing.
- New hobbies you've been wanting to try.
- Things that naturally grab your attention or make time fly by.

Examples could include painting, hiking, writing, gardening, learning an instrument, photography, etc.

Step 3: Review and Reflect on Your List

Once you've listed 10-20 activities, take a moment to review the list. Circle or highlight the ones that resonate most with you right now. Consider which activities make you feel most energized or have a deeper personal meaning.

Step 4: Choose One Activity to Explore

From the highlighted items, select one activity or hobby that you're most excited to explore further. This choice should be something that feels both fun and challenging, providing you with the opportunity to grow creatively.

Step 5: Schedule Regular Time for It

Dedicate a specific block of time to regularly engage in this activity. Whether it's 15 minutes a day or a couple of hours on the weekend, consistency is key. Use your calendar or planner to schedule these sessions as if they were important appointments.

Step 6: Engage Fully and Observe Your Experience

When you engage in the activity, immerse yourself in it completely. Pay attention to how you feel during the process. Are you losing track of time? Does it feel like you're in a state of flow, where creativity comes naturally?

Step 7: Reflect and Adjust

After each session, reflect on how the activity is impacting your creativity and passion. Are you enjoying it? Does it make you feel more energized? If so, continue. If not, feel free to adjust and try another activity from your list.

By following these steps, you'll gradually find an activity that helps you tap into your flow state, fueling your creativity and passion.

What activities make me feel most alive
and engaged?

_____

_____

_____

_____

What are my creative strengths and how can I express them
more fully?

_____

_____

_____

_____

> **"My ADHD allows me to hyper-focus when I'm passionate about something. It's challenging, but it's part of what makes me, me." — Lisa Ling**

Chapter 7

CREATING A LIFE YOU LOVE

Understanding that you're not alone on this journey is essential. ADHD affects millions of women around the world, with many remaining undiagnosed or misdiagnosed until later in life.

The challenges for women with ADHD are often shaped by societal expectations, gender roles, and the juggling of multiple responsibilities. It's common to feel overwhelmed, scattered, and unsure about the next steps.

Yet, within the chaos, there's a spark of resilience—a strength that comes from facing adversity and persisting. Women with ADHD often possess a blend of creativity, passion, and intuition. They have a zest for life, a thirst for knowledge, and a strong desire to make a meaningful impact. When these traits are recognized and channeled, they can become powerful tools for building a fulfilling life.

Embracing this journey means recognizing both the challenges and strengths that come with ADHD. It's about understanding that your brain is wired differently, but that difference can be a strength. It offers a unique perspective on the world, one that is incredibly valuable when fully embraced.

This process is not about **"fixing"** yourself or trying to conform to a standard that doesn't fit you. It's about accepting yourself with all your quirks, imperfections, and unique abilities.

It's about working with your brain, not against it, and finding strategies that help you thrive in various aspects of life.

Part of this involves learning more about ADHD and how it specifically affects you. This could mean seeking information, resources, and support from professionals, therapists, coaches, or support groups. It also means recognizing your triggers, patterns, and developing personalized coping mechanisms.

But managing ADHD is only part of the equation. It's also about celebrating your strengths, exploring your passions, and finding ways to express your unique talents. Whether it's starting a new career, pursuing a creative project, or simply living in alignment with your values, the goal is to build a life that feels authentic and fulfilling.

Having a support system is crucial. This could include family, friends, mentors, or other women with ADHD who understand your experiences and can offer encouragement and advice. Finding a community where you feel understood and accepted without judgment can make all the difference.

Self-compassion is another key aspect of embracing your journey. Many women with ADHD struggle with self-criticism and negative self-talk. It's important to be kind to yourself, acknowledge your efforts, and forgive yourself for any mistakes or setbacks. Progress isn't always linear, and there will be ups and downs along the way.

SELF-COMPASSION

Self-compassion is the antidote to that harsh inner critic. It's not about making excuses or letting yourself off the hook.

Rather, it's about treating yourself with the same kindness and understanding you would offer to a friend in need. It's acknowledging your humanity—flaws, mistakes, and all—and realizing that those imperfections are a part of life.

For women with ADHD, self-compassion is especially vital. Why? Because the symptoms of ADHD—forgetfulness, impulsivity, difficulty following through—often lead to a painful cycle of self-blame and shame.

You might get frustrated with yourself for missing a deadline, forgetting an appointment, or misplacing your keys again. This constant self-criticism doesn't just drain your mental health; it also undermines your ability to manage ADHD effectively.

When you're stuck in a loop of self-blame, it's hard to stay motivated or hopeful. You may start believing that you're incapable of change, destined to be disorganized and overwhelmed.

But self-compassion shifts that narrative. It reminds you that your struggles don't define your worth or abilities—they're simply the result of how your brain works. With the right strategies and tools, you can learn to navigate these challenges.

So, how do you cultivate self-compassion? It begins with awareness. Start paying attention to your inner dialogue.

How often do you criticize or judge yourself? And how often do you speak to yourself with kindness? When you catch yourself engaging in negative self-talk, challenge those thoughts. Instead of saying, **"I'm so stupid for forgetting the dry cleaning,"** try reframing it: **"I'm human, and sometimes I forget things. It's okay."**

Mindfulness is another powerful practice for cultivating self-compassion. Mindfulness is simply being present in the moment without judgment. Instead of getting stuck in past regrets or worrying about the future, you observe your thoughts and feelings as they are—without letting them sweep you away.

Meditation is one way to practice mindfulness, but it doesn't have to be intimidating. Even a few minutes of focused breathing can make a big difference. Sit comfortably, close your eyes, and concentrate on your breath. Feel the rise and fall of your chest as you inhale and exhale. If your mind wanders (which it will), gently guide your focus back to your breath without criticism.

Positive affirmations are also a helpful tool. Create affirming statements about yourself, such as **"I am worthy of love and respect,"** or **"I am capable of achieving my goals."** Repeat these throughout the day.

While it may feel awkward at first, these affirmations can gradually reprogram your mindset, helping you replace self-criticism with self-acceptance.

By practicing these tools, you'll begin to shift how you relate to yourself—moving away from blame and toward understanding, from criticism to compassion. This gentle, more forgiving relationship with yourself can profoundly change how you manage ADHD and create a more hopeful, empowered path forward.

YOUR ADHD ROADMAP

Congratulations on reaching this final chapter! But as you know by now, this isn't the end—it's the beginning of an exciting new chapter in your life, one where you take charge of your ADHD and channel it in ways that allow you to thrive.

Together, we've explored the complications of ADHD in women over 40, highlighting the hidden struggles and helping you reframe your narrative.

You've been equipped with practical tools to manage focus, organization, emotional well-being, and relationships.

Most importantly, you've learned to embrace the unique strengths your ADHD brings—creativity, resilience, and passion—and build a support system that understands and uplifts you.

109

Now, the next step is yours: creating your personalized ADHD roadmap.

Remember, ADHD doesn't look the same for everyone. Your challenges and strengths are as unique as you are, and that's why your roadmap should reflect your specific goals, needs, and preferences. There's no "normal" standard to live up to—just the best version of life that works for you.

Here are some questions to guide your journey:

What are your main challenges?
Where do you struggle most—focus, time management, emotional regulation, or relationships? Identifying these can help you prioritize what needs the most attention.

What are your strengths?
How can you use your creativity, intuition, or empathy to your advantage? Understanding your strengths allows you to leverage them in overcoming obstacles.

What resources are available to you?

Are there professionals, coaches, or support groups who can offer additional guidance? Building a network of support will help you stay accountable and inspired.

What are your personal and professional goals?

What kind of life do you want to design? Do you want more balance, fulfillment, or creative freedom? Your roadmap should align with these aspirations.

There is no one-size-fits-all approach to managing ADHD. Your roadmap will likely evolve as you try new strategies and learn what works for you. Be patient with yourself as you experiment. If one tool doesn't work, don't hesitate to try another. Celebrate the small victories, and learn from the setbacks.

KEY TAKEAWAYS
FROM THIS BOOK

As you venture forward, keep these important reminders close to heart:

ADHD is not a flaw.

It's a neurological difference that brings its own set of strengths and challenges. Embrace your neurodiversity as a gift, not a deficit.

You are not alone.

Millions of women live with ADHD, many of them undiagnosed for years. Seek out a community of women who understand your experience and can offer support and empathy.

Knowledge is power.

The more you learn about ADHD, the better equipped you'll be to make informed decisions about treatment, self-care, and personal development.

Self-compassion is essential.

Be kind to yourself when you stumble. Everyone makes mistakes, and progress isn't always linear. Celebrate every step forward, no matter how small.

Your roadmap is unique.

There is no predefined path. Your journey is yours alone, and your personalized ADHD plan should reflect what works best for you and your dreams.

There is hope.

ADHD doesn't define your limits—it shapes how you experience the world. With the right strategies and support, you can create a life that is both meaningful and fulfilling.

EXERCISES

Writing a Letter of Self-Compassion

This exercise guides you through the process of writing a letter of self-compassion, allowing you to embrace your journey and practice kindness toward yourself. Follow these steps:

Step 1: Find a Quiet Space
- Purpose: Create a peaceful, distraction-free environment.
- Action: Choose a calm spot where you can focus, like a cozy corner or a quiet room.

Step 2: Reflect on Your Struggles
- Purpose: Acknowledge the challenges you've faced.
- Action: Take a few moments to think about the hardships, setbacks, or obstacles you've encountered recently or in the past.
- Tip: Be honest and gentle with yourself. This is a time to reflect, not to judge.

114

Step 3: Acknowledge Your Emotions

- Purpose: Validate your feelings.
- Action: Write down the emotions associated with these struggles. It could be frustration, sadness, fear, or disappointment. Allow yourself to feel without minimizing your experience.
- Tip: Use phrases like "It's okay to feel this way," or "These emotions are valid."

Step 4: Affirm Your Strengths

- Purpose: Recognize the qualities that have helped you through difficult times.
- Action: List your strengths—whether it's resilience, creativity, persistence, or empathy—that have enabled you to cope with or overcome challenges.
- Tip: Be specific. For example, "I handled a tough conversation at work with patience," or "I've managed to stay hopeful despite uncertainty."

Step 5: Remind Yourself of Your Worth

- Purpose: Reinforce your value, independent of challenges.
- Action: Write statements reminding yourself that you are deserving of love, acceptance, and kindness. Emphasize that your worth is not determined by your struggles.
- Tip: Use phrases like "I am enough just as I am," or "I am worthy of love, no matter what."

Step 6: Offer Yourself Encouragement

- Purpose: Provide yourself with compassionate support for the future.
- Action: End your letter by offering words of encouragement. Remind yourself that you are on a unique journey, and that growth is a continual process. Write what you would say to a friend going through similar challenges.
- Tip: Examples could be "I am proud of how far I've come, and I trust I will continue to grow," or "I have the strength to navigate whatever comes my way."

116

Step 7: Read Your Letter Aloud

- Purpose: Deepen the connection to your self-compassion.
- Action: After writing, read your letter out loud. Hear the kindness in your words and let it resonate with you emotionally.
- Tip: If you feel comfortable, you can re-read this letter whenever you need a reminder of your resilience and worth.

Step 8: Keep the Letter as a Reminder

- Purpose: Create a tangible reminder of your journey.
- Action: Save the letter in a place where you can revisit it, such as a journal or a special box. Return to it whenever you feel discouraged or need to practice self-compassion.

This exercise is a powerful way to reconnect with your inner strength, remind yourself of your value, and embrace the journey toward creating a life you love.

What are my biggest fears and insecurities about having ADHD?

_____

_____

_____

_____

_____

What are my long-term goals for personal growth and well-being, and how can I create a roadmap to achieve them?

_____

_____

_____

_____

THANK YOU NOTE

Hi Dearie's,

Thank you so much for picking up ADHD After 40 Workbook for Women. I truly hope this book gives you the support and tools you need on your journey with ADHD.

If it has helped you, I'd really appreciate it if you could leave a review on Amazon. Your feedback means the world to me and helps others find this resource too.

Thank you again for your trust and support!

Warmly,
Ava Park.

Made in the USA
Middletown, DE
08 October 2024

62185185R00071